JAPAN

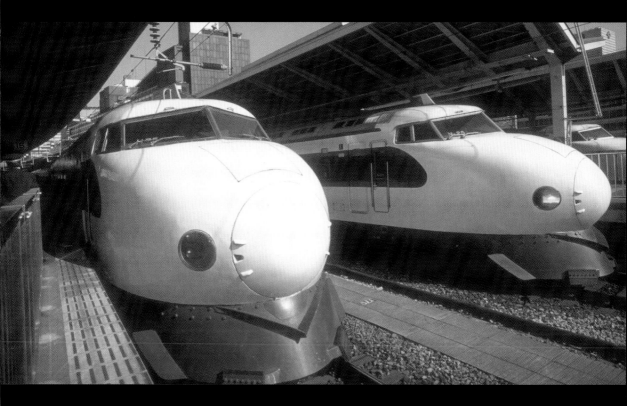

ROBERT CASE

Evans

TITLES IN THE COUNTRIES OF THE WORLD SERIES:
BRAZIL • FRANCE • JAPAN • KENYA • UNITED KINGDOM • USA

Published by Evans Brothers Limited
2A Portman Mansions
Chiltern Street
London W1U 6NR

Produced for Evans Brothers Limited by
Monkey Puzzle Media Limited
Gissing's Farm, Fressingfield
Suffolk IP21 5SH

VISIT OUR WEBSITE
www.evansbooks.co.uk
Evans

First published 2002
© copyright Evans Brothers 2002
© copyright in the text Robert Case 2002

British Library Cataloguing in Publication Data
Japan. - (Countries of the world)
1.Japan - Juvenile literature
I.Title
952

ISBN 0 237 52271 3

Editor: Katie Orchard
Designer: Jane Hawkins
Map artwork by Peter Bull
Charts and graphs produced by Alex Pang

Endpapers (front): The sprawling Tokyo skyline.
(back): The steep walk to Mount Fuji.
Title page: Two *shinkansen* trains, ready to depart.
Imprint and Contents page: Lilies on the water in
the Zen Temple gardens at Ryoan-ji in Kyoto.

The author would like to thank Professor Martin Brennan of
Beppu University and Kenji Murakami, formerly of Keio University
(Tokyo), who helped in the preparation of this book.
The book is dedicated to the memory of the author's father, who
died during its preparation.

All photographs taken by Robert Case except for the following, which were kindly supplied by: Corbis 13 (Michael S.
Yamashita), 16 (Michael S. Yamashita), 26 (top/Michael S. Yamashita); Corbis Digital Stock endpapers (back and front), 10, 14,
19; Impact 33 (bottom/Philip Gordon), 34 (Philip Gordon), 50–51 (bottom/Philip Gordon); RCP Images title page, 23, 24, 25
(top), 26 (bottom), 46, 57; Still Pictures 39 (Ron Giling); Toyota Motor Manufacturing (UK) Limited 36 (top).

The Japanese flag. The Japanese name for Japan is *Nihon-Koku*, which means 'land of the rising sun'. The red disk on the flag represents the sun.

One of the miniature islands of the sacred site at Matsushima, Honshu.

Japan is a country of many contrasts. Economically it is the second most powerful country in the world, yet little is known of it in the West. Japan was a loser in the Second World War but has made a miraculous recovery. It is one of the world's leaders in technology but it also retains much of its distinctive traditional culture. All this comes from a relatively modest-sized country situated on the edge of the Pacific Ocean.

ISLANDS AND MOUNTAINS

Japan is made up of four principal islands, Honshu, Hokkaido, Kyushu and Shikoku, and nearly 7,000 smaller islands, situated between 20°25' N and 45°33' N. These islands form part of a geologically active island arc containing many volcanoes and struck regularly by earth tremors. A line of mountains runs through the interior of all four main islands and dominates the country.

In such a mountainous country, areas of flat land are limited and have to be intensively used. This can be seen on several levels, in high-density urban living, the large number of high-rise buildings, and farms that are small and intensively worked, with paddy fields tucked into urban areas and terraces cut into hillsides.

JAPAN'S PEOPLE

With so little available low-lying land, Japan's basins are densely populated. The largest of these, the Kanto Plain, has an area of over 32,000km² with a population of 38.5 million people living there. It contains the nation's capital, Tokyo, and many other large cities, including Yokohama. There are also a number of small, isolated basins and lowlands that house important cities such as Kyoto, Nara, Hiroshima and Okayama.

The Japanese are a single ethnic group but there are a small number of minority groups living in Japan, including the *burakumin*, Koreans and Ainu (see page 22). Much of Japanese culture has been influenced by Asian cultures and its written language is derived from Chinese. However, in more recent times, with its increasing importance in the world economy, Japan has been influenced by some aspects of Western culture, and traditional and modern lifestyles are often seen side by side.

The Tokyo skyline. Over 12 million people live in the capital city's urban sprawl.

People are Japan's greatest asset, but the Japanese are having fewer children.

PHYSICAL CHALLENGES

Japan's coastline is heavily indented with many small peninsulas, capes, bays and inlets. Shallow waters have often been reclaimed from the sea to extend the amount of land available for farming, industry and settlement.

The physical environment of Japan has proven a challenge to Japanese ingenuity and contributed to its distinctive society. All communications such as road and rail networks are expensive to construct in a mountainous environment, yet despite the limitations of the landscape the Japanese treat it with great spiritual reverence.

KEY DATA

Official Name:	Japan
Area:	377,855km²
Population:	126.5 million
Official Language:	Japanese
Main Cities:	Tokyo (capital), Kobe, Yokohama, Osaka, Nagoya, Sapporo, Kyoto and Fukuoka
GDP per capita:	US$24,898*
Currency:	Yen
Exchange Rate:	US$1 = 133 yen £1 = 188 yen (January 2002)

* Calculated on Purchasing Power Parity basis

Mount Fuji, Japan's national emblem, is a spectacular tourist attraction.

Japan is located in one of the most geologically active regions in the world. Its striking landscape is peppered with dozens of active volcanoes, youthful mountain ranges and scores of hot springs. These natural features combine to make Japan a beautiful country, but it is also one of ever-present danger – the landscape is regularly rocked by earthquakes and flooded by giant waves called tsunami.

Japan is drained by short, steep and rapidly flowing rivers – the longest, the Shinano, which flows into the Sea of Japan at Niigata, is only 367km long. The steep nature of these rivers makes them prone to flooding during the rainy seasons and many of the lower reaches are protected by elaborate and expensive flood-defence schemes.

FORMATION OF THE ISLAND ARC

Japan is located on the boundaries between four of the earth's tectonic plates. Significantly the Pacific plate is converging on the Eurasian plate and sinking beneath it. This movement is not very smooth and can lead to sudden jolts that result in earthquakes. As the Pacific plate descends, surface deposits are scraped off and deformed. The oceanic crust eventually melts and rises towards the surface as lava, where much of it erupts in a large number of active and dangerous volcanoes. These volcanic outpourings combine with the scraped-off sediments to create a mountainous chain of islands, an island arc.

LANDSCAPE FEATURES

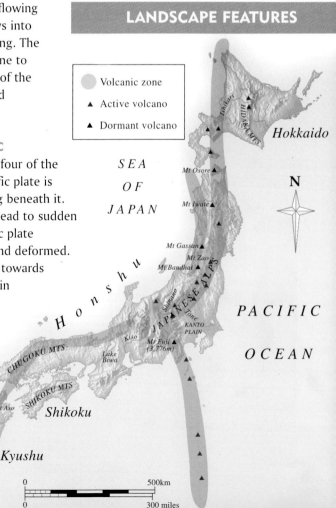

Volcanic zone
▲ Active volcano
▲ Dormant volcano

Hokkaido

SEA
OF
JAPAN

Mt Osore ▲

Mt Iwate ▲

Mt Gassan ▲
Mt Zao ▲
Mt Bandhai ▲

N

Hon s h u

JAPANESE ALPS

KANTO
PLAIN

PACIFIC

OCEAN

Kiso

Mt Fuji ▲
(3,776m)

Lake
Biwa

CHUGOKU MTS

SHIKOKU MTS

Shikoku

RYUKYU
ISLANDS

Mt Aso
Mt Unzen ▲

KYUSHU MTS

Mt Sakurajima ▲

Kyushu

EAST
CHINA
SEA

Okinawa

0   500km

0   300 miles

The most famous volcano in Japan is Mount Fuji or *Fuji-san*, as it is known locally, which rises to 3,776m. The sheer size and near-perfect conical shape of the volcano make it a dramatic sight that can be seen as far away as Tokyo. Mount Fuji is a popular tourist destination and many people climb to its summit each year. The volcano last erupted in 1707 and has been dormant ever since. However, in August 2000, scientists detected low-frequency tremors under Mount Fuji. These are being closely studied and prompted sufficient alarm to cause a full-scale emergency rescue practice-run in June 2001.

All Japan's active volcanoes are carefully monitored. Warnings enable early evacuation, and important infrastructure (transport and communications networks and utilities) in these areas has been designed to minimise damage. In some areas, spillways have been built to channel lava away from settlements. Japan also has many hot springs or *onzen*. They provide a useful source of geothermal

Beppu's famous thermal springs are hot enough to boil eggs.

power for the country. The hot springs are a major tourist attraction as well, with visitors wishing to sample the healing and therapeutic qualities of the thermal waters. Beppu and Yufuin are popular spas, attracting visitors from all over Japan.

CASE STUDY
MOUNT ASO

Smoke rises from the crater of Nakedake, one of Mount Aso's active peaks.

One area of high volcanic activity is the volcano complex of Mount Aso, in Kyushu. There have been many eruptions here and one of the principal peaks, Nakedake, continues to belch sulphurous gases and occasional volcanic bombs. Although visitors can access the edge of the crater, there are substantial protection measures in place to avoid any danger. The road leading to the volcano has a security gate at some distance from the crater, so that the road can be closed to traffic in an emergency. When the gases are particularly toxic, visitors are provided with face masks. Around the crater are bomb shelters, intended to provide emergency protection in the event of a sudden eruption. Despite these precautions, visitors are rewarded with an awesome sight. Sulphurous mists rise amid a colourful array of old lavas, and the eerie, steel-blue crater lake almost glows at a temperature of about 90°C.

NATURAL HAZARDS

Japan's location makes it one of the most hazardous countries on earth. The greatest threats come from earthquakes and tsunami. Japan experiences as many as 7,500 tremors a year, 150 in Tokyo alone. Most of these pass unnoticed, but a number are significant. Since the famous 1923 Kanto earthquake, Japan has experienced 16 earthquakes or tsunami, seven of which have killed 1,000 people or more. The last significant tsunami, on 12 July 1993, was triggered by an earthquake measuring 7.8 on the Richter scale, just offshore from south-west Hokkaido. The resulting tidal wave reached a height of 30m and was travelling at around 500 kilometres per hour when it hit the small island of Okushiri. It caused extensive damage, killed 230 people and destroyed 601 buildings.

Flood defences protect the population, but they can detract from a river's natural beauty.

TYPHOONS

Typhoons occur mainly between August and October. They are characterised by violent winds of up to 200 kilometres per hour and intense rainfall that may exceed 300mm in a day. These typhoons originate in the Pacific Ocean and affect mainly eastern and south-western Honshu, north-west Kyushu and the Nansei Islands in the south. Typhoons can cause considerable damage to buildings, but it is often the damage to agriculture that is more serious as the winds can flatten crops.

Typhoons can also trigger floods. Japan's short, steep rivers originate in upland basins in the mountains. Peak flows can develop rapidly, leading to flooding in the heavily urbanised lowland areas. Japan has spent vast sums of money on flood defences and as a result few Japanese rivers retain their natural features. Peak flows combined with high tides and onshore winds can often result in coastal flooding. Again extensive defences have been erected to combat this, often turning the shoreline into a concrete barrier rather than a natural beach. Heavy rainfall and snowfall can also trigger landslides and avalanches, and these regularly cause local damage in the mountains and nearby areas, although relatively few people are killed.

Modern high-rise apartment blocks are now built to resist the effects of earthquakes.

CASE STUDY
KOBE EARTHQUAKE

The most recent significant earthquake was that which struck Kobe at 5.46 on the morning of 17 January 1995. It registered 7.3 on the Richter scale and caused widespread destruction. Traditional wooden houses with tiled roofs were particularly vulnerable, as were buildings that had been constructed before the introduction of shock-proof foundations in the 1960s. At the height of the disaster, a million homes lost their water supply, 110,000 homes were without electricity and 900,000 had no gas supply.

In total, 500,000 buildings were damaged or destroyed, many of them by fires ignited by overturned kerosene heaters. There was also extensive damage to the port facilities, roads such as the Hanshin Expressway and a section of the Tokaido *shinkansen* (the high-speed railway network). The official death toll was 6,430, and 43,000 people were injured. Kobe has since made a remarkable recovery – most of its infrastructure has been restored, its buildings rebuilt and its port and economy are now fully functional.

Cars and buildings lay in ruins after the terrible earthquake in Kobe.

DEALING WITH DISASTER

Japan has invested heavily in the prevention and prediction of disasters, and also in the minimisation of their effects. An extensive system of hi-tech equipment such as seismographs can detect tremors from earthquakes and volcanic activity on land and at sea. Although these are unable to predict earthquakes, they can give warning of tsunami. The data can also be fed immediately to organisations such as gas companies, enabling systems to be shut down to minimise the risk of fires. Transport networks and emergency services can also be alerted. In addition, sophisticated monitoring provides forecasts so that people can be evacuated safely from areas at risk of flooding or landslides, and all hotels and public buildings provide advice on what to do in an emergency. Although these precautions cannot prevent disasters, they can at least reduce the impact of such catastrophes.

CLIMATE

Japan experiences a monsoon climate. This is a seasonal change of wind and air mass. In the winter, when levels of sunlight are low, an intensely cold air mass builds up over East Asia. The air sinks and creates an area of high pressure, making the winds blow away from it and outwards over the Sea of Japan. As they move, the cold, dry winds pick up moisture from the sea, forming cloud – this can bring heavy snowfall to the west of Japan and the central mountains. By the time it reaches the Pacific Ocean, however, the air has lost most of its moisture and so this side of the country experiences relatively dry winters. Even on the Sea of Japan side snow does not fall all the time. For much of the winter, Japan has dry and sunny but cold weather, particularly in the north, in places such as Hokkaido and northern Honshu. Further south in Kyushu and Shikoku temperatures are milder.

In spring the high pressure begins to weaken. This is often a time of very pleasant weather in Japan. Clear, bright skies and rising temperatures encourage the cherry trees to blossom. This welcome splash of colour is cherished and celebrated throughout the whole country.

Cherry-blossom time in Japan is reported in all the media and is a cause of national celebration.

Rising temperatures lead to rising air and unstable conditions of low pressure. This area of low pressure draws warm, moist oceanic air to it, borne on south-easterly winds from the tropics. The moist air forms cloud as it moves over Japan and the rainy season arrives in early to mid-June. During the rainy season many days start out dry and sunny, but as the heat builds up dense cloud develops, leading to heavy downpours and thunderstorms. Such intense rainfall can lead to flooding and landslides. Temperatures often exceed 25°C in the afternoon (often 30°C in Tokyo in the early afternoon) and humidity is very high.

Towards the end of June the inter-tropical front that is the main focus of the rainfall moves north-westwards, leaving most of Japan immersed in warm, moist oceanic air. Temperatures at this time of year tend to be high and it is very humid.

In September the front moves south-eastwards again and Japan experiences a second rainy season, which is associated with typhoons. This gives way to a dry, warm autumn before the return of winter.

There are considerable regional variations to this general weather pattern. Hokkaido, being further north, is colder throughout the year and the monsoon effect is less marked. By contrast Okinawa, which is far to the south, has a sub-tropical climate. The Pacific coast is much more affected by the monsoon and the typhoons, while the Sea of Japan coast is more prone to winter snow and less to the monsoon. Temperatures are generally cooler throughout the year in the mountains where there are heavy snowfalls in winter, ideal for winter sports – indeed Japan hosted the Winter Olympics in Sapporo in 1972 and at Nagano in 1998.

The climatic changes are a source of reverence for the Japanese, who hold festivals at various significant seasons such as the cherry-blossom season.

The snow-capped Japanese Alps form a backdrop to much of Honshu's urban landscape.

TEMPERATURE AND RAINFALL

TOKYO

Temp (°C) / Rainfall (mm)

SAPPORO

Temp (°C) / Rainfall (mm)

HIROSHIMA

Temp (°C) / Rainfall (mm)

FUKUOKA

Temp (°C) / Rainfall (mm)

KEY:

Temp (°C)

Rainfall (mm)

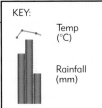

Kyushu's sub-tropical climate is ideal for growing sun-loving crops such as these daikon radishes.

NATIONAL REGIONS

As well as being a country made up of many islands, Japan can be divided up according to its eight national regions – Chubu, Kinki, Chugoku, Kyushu, Shikoku, Kanto, Tohoku and Hokkaido. Hokkaido is very mountainous, and the region experiences cold winters and mild summers. Hokkaido is sparsely populated – only 5.7 million people live there, on 21 per cent of Japan's land area. Farming is of major importance here.

Tohoku occupies northern Honshu. The north of this region is still relatively remote but in the south it benefits from the eastward growth of the Tokaido Megalopolis (a massive urban area that stretches from Tokyo through to Kobe). Tohoku is an important area of rice cultivation – 25 per cent of the country's output comes from this region.

Kanto incorporates Japan's principal lowland. For this reason, Kanto has been important to both agriculture and industry. Today the region is characterised by the great urban sprawl that houses a host of large cities including Tokyo and Yokohama.

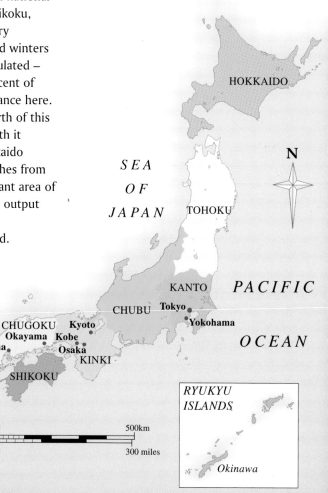

The south of Chubu forms the central part of the Tokaido Megalopolis and the centre of the region contains the Japanese Alps. To the north lie small lowlands around Niigata, another important area for rice growing.

Kinki encompasses the western end of the megalopolis and is host to three of Japan's great cities, Osaka, Kobe and the ancient capital of Japan, Kyoto.

Chugoku occupies the western end of Honshu. In the south it houses vast cities such as Hiroshima and Okayama – the north by contrast is one of the least developed, poorest areas in Japan.

Shikoku has a mountainous interior. The region's population is concentrated along its coastal strips, particularly those bordering the Inland Sea, some of which are very industrialised. Shikoku was quite isolated in the past, but new bridges are increasing its communication links and the area is becoming popular for tourism.

The western coast of Kyushu boasts some magnificent beaches, popular with people who live in Fukuoka.

Kyushu has a mountainous interior, which includes many active volcanoes such as Sakurajima, Aso and Unzen. Much of it has a sub-tropical climate, which provides ideal growing conditions for crops such as oranges. It also has an important area of industry in the north, as well as a range of hi-tech industries scattered around the coast.

COASTAL DIFFERENCES

Japan can be divided between the Sea of Japan side and the Pacific side. There are differences in climate, culture and economy between these two sides of Japan's four main islands. The Sea of Japan side is more prone to cold climatic influences from Asia, while the Pacific side is warmer. The Sea of Japan side has an ancient culture reflecting links with the continent. The Pacific side, however, has grown more rapidly in the last 50 years and it is there that modern Japanese culture is centred, particularly in Tokyo.

Young people in Japan sometimes question the country's traditional values.

Japanese culture is distinctive, partly due to a period of prolonged isolation from the rest of the world under the shoguns (1603–1868). During this time Japan evolved its own customs and traditions. The country retained many of its traditional values into the twentieth century and its economic success has often been attributed in part to these values. However, more recently Japan has been influenced by the rest of the world and there are signs that the culture is changing.

Social values in Japan are linked in part to religion, and include strong family and social ties. Traditionally the Japanese had large extended families with several generations living under one roof, sharing a communal lifestyle. The cooperative and helpful nature of the Japanese is one of the nation's key characteristics and can be seen on many levels of society. Examples range from a passing stranger who is willing to miss her train to ensure that a tourist catches the right one, to the high level of courtesy demonstrated by shop assistants. Such attitudes are also an important feature in the workplace, where committees are established to address managerial issues and include staff from all levels within the company. At the start of work, many workforces share in communal warming-up exercises, and few Japanese would go home leaving a task half-finished or a customer without a response.

Whilst these attitudes have contributed to Japan's success, recently many traditional Japanese values have come under pressure as economic circumstances have changed. In the 1990s recession created unemployment and many companies had to change their work practices. Since then, there has been a growing divorce rate and a loosening of family ties. There has also been an increase in some types of crime, although Japan remains one of the most crime-free countries in the world.

There are 40,000 shrines in Japan, many tucked into urban back streets such as this one in Kyoto.

The Japanese are not unique in facing the challenge of change but their difficulties may be more fundamental. The success of the country since 1945 has been phenomenal, and that success was built as much on shared social values as on hi-tech inventiveness. Japan's recession, and the redundancies it has caused, have had a more serious effect there than they would have in countries more used to unemployment.

RELIGION

Japan has many religions. Shintoism, Japan's most ancient religion, is a mixture of early South-east Asian beliefs. The religion has divinities known as *kami*, who are able to bestow blessings, for example for a happy marriage. In the sixth century Buddhism was introduced to Japan from Korea. The religion's elaborate style of art and architecture made it attractive to the imperial court at the time, and Buddhism became the official state religion. Buddhism spread easily throughout Japan and a number of sects developed; the best-known in the West is Zen. Christianity was introduced to Japan by the Portuguese in 1549 and gained some popularity. Today there is no dominant religion in Japan and, in fact, many Japanese practise several religions.

THE SHOGUNS

Traditional Japanese architecture, such as this temple, dates back to shogun rule.

From 1603 to 1868 Japan was ruled by military leaders known as shoguns, who believed that foreigners posed a threat to the stability of the state. Japan closed itself to all external influences: foreigners were not allowed to enter the country, and the Japanese were not permitted to leave. After a number of attempts by the British, Dutch and Americans to open up Japan to trade, Commander Perry of the US Navy finally negotiated the Treaty of Kanagawa in 1854. Internal strife encouraged by Dutch, French, British and US actions led to the shoguns being overthrown in 1868. The new regime restored the authority of the emperor, who was the 14-year-old Mitsushito. Real power lay in the hands of reformers, who set up a series of political, social and economic reforms that would transform Japan. This period is known as the Meiji Restoration. When Japan opened its doors to the rest of the world, it was eager to catch up with the progress of the West. A phenomenal period of economic and population growth followed.

A COMPACT CULTURE

Japanese society and culture are incredibly compact. It is often assumed that this is a response to the scarcity of level land, yet the Japanese appreciation of all things in miniature has a long history. It expresses itself in Bonsai (the art of growing tiny trees), miniature electronic goods and tiny gardens, among many other things. Even Japanese apartment blocks have small, space-saving flats. Local shops are also closely packed and specialised, and these are supplemented by *yatori* or movable street stalls. There are few pavements and even fewer private garages – instead cars are stacked up in tiered car parks.

LIMITED SPACE

This compactness requires very careful organisation. In agriculture this has traditionally been expressed through multiple cropping (growing a range of crops in one area) and carefully organised rice cultivation. Community groups act together to make

Despite its size, Tokyo's streets are cleaner than most Western cities.

neighbourhoods work efficiently and harmoniously in relatively small spaces. Although Japan's cities have not generally been planned, there are often neighbourhood associations, which meet to plan events. They try to organise life as well as possible for all residents.

Many homes in Japan are small and compact, like these apartments in Beppu.

Japanese parks and gardens are immaculate.
This grass is being cut by hand.

A well-ordered and organised environment is important to the Japanese. For example, visitors often notice the neatly trimmed fields, weed-free roadsides and clean city streets. Buildings have scrubbed store fronts and homes are clutter-free.

A curious feature of Japan's landscape is its relative lack of any real specialisation. Whilst there is some variation in types of agriculture across the country, much of the Japanese landscape is diversified – a range of crops are grown close to each other on tiny parcels of land. Farms lie alongside other land uses such as factories, and paddy fields can be found amid the urban areas – even in central Tokyo there are some 18km^2 of farm plots.

A Society of Many Layers

Another characteristic of Japanese society is its tiered or vertically layered nature. In the countryside are terraces that cut into the hillsides; in the cities are the multiple levels of roads and railways, and the vertical layers of activity within high-rise buildings. There are underground railways and shopping malls, and shops jostle for space on street level beneath high-rise apartment blocks, while rooftop leisure activities take place above them.

KEEPING JAPAN CLEAN

Japan is a nation obsessed with cleanliness and order. There is a huge range of hygienic products available, such as antiseptic pencils and pens, cleaning chemicals, electronic toilets and face masks to prevent colds spreading. Traditional customs, such as ritual bathing and the removal of shoes before entering a house or shrine, also reflect the Japanese concern with cleanliness and hygiene.

Electronic toilets even have heated seats!

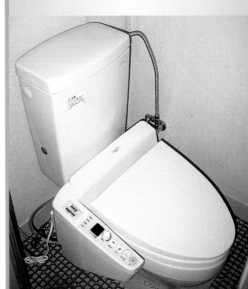

Limited flat land for construction leads to high urban population densities.

JAPAN'S POPULATION

Japan's present population numbers over 126 million. Most people are ethnically Japanese. Whilst there has always been migration within the country there has been little immigration, despite Japan's attraction as a wealthy 'honeypot'. As a result, there is very little diversity among the people of Japan. There are only three significant minority groups – the Ainu, the *burakumin* and the Koreans (see box).

Japan's population is distributed unevenly across the country, with the greatest concentration of people living in the Pacific Belt (see pages 34–35). There are several reasons why the population density varies so greatly across Japan. Only 15 per cent of the land is suitable for building on, so settlements have been limited to a relatively small area. There is also a lack of agricultural land, so farming is concentrated in a limited number of plains around the coast. The climate is also an important factor in population distribution, as the east and south are warmer and more attractive to settlement. These areas also provide convenient trade links to other Pacific countries, and so are popular industrial locations. Japan has a number of active volcanoes and areas prone to extreme flooding, and wherever

MINORITY GROUPS

The Ainu were the original inhabitants of Hokkaido and once had their own culture and language. Today there are very few Ainu left – officially about 15,000. The *burakumin* (meaning 'community people') are not racially distinguishable from the Japanese. In the time of the shoguns they were an underclass, outcasts who performed jobs that were deemed to be unclean. Today there are roughly 3 million or so *burakumin* living in Japan. Although the *burakumin* now have full legal rights, they still suffer some discrimination. There are also about 700,000 Koreans living in Japan, many of whom were born there. Many come from families that were brought to Japan as labourers during the Japanese occupation of Korea between 1910 and 1945.

With fewer children being born, the average age of Japan's population is rising.

POPULATION, 1950–2050

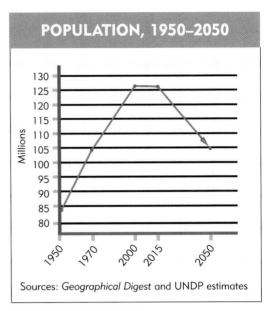

Sources: *Geographical Digest* and UNDP estimates

POPULATION DENSITY

Persons/km²

Above 1,328

664 — 1,328

332 — 663

116 — 331

Below 116

possible people have chosen to avoid these areas for settlement. The distribution of natural resources has also played an important role in the development of certain areas, particularly during the nineteenth century when coalfields and other resources attracted settlement to places such as north-east Kyushu.

Historical factors, such as the movements of people and the types and locations of governments, which have included Imperial and Shogunate regimes as well as democratic ones, have also influenced population density. Nara, Tokyo and Kyoto have all acted as capitals at one time or another.

All these factors have led to a distinctive pattern of population distribution. Most people live in the Tokaido Megalopolis and the core urban areas continue to grow rapidly. More recently, there have been some marked population increases in areas such as Sendai and southern Kyushu, but much of Japan still has population densities below the national average.

HOUSING

Most urban development in Japan is on its limited areas of flat land. This has led to very high population densities in some areas – in 1990, 63.2 per cent of the population lived on only 3.2 per cent of Japan's land surface. Competition for land is fierce, and as a result house prices have spiralled.

Given the high cost of housing, the Japanese have to borrow heavily to purchase their homes (sometimes as much as 13 times their annual income). This has led to mortgages spread over several generations. It has also contributed to the high cost of living in Tokyo, which is one of the most expensive cities in the world. Surprisingly, home ownership remains popular in Japan – 60.3 per cent of the population owned their own homes in 1993.

Japanese houses tend to be small. A typical house has 4.79 rooms, 93.45m² of space and 0.59 persons a room. In Tokyo the figures are lower still – 3.5 rooms, 63.6m² and 0.67 persons per room.

Many Japanese people live in flats or small apartments and have to make intensive use of the limited space. Every available corner of

These people have sat down to eat a typical Japanese meal in traditional surroundings.

a Japanese apartment is utilised. Moveable screens (called *fusuma*) are used to divide up the rooms into different areas, kitchens are often in part of the living room and washing machines jostle for space in bathrooms. Most modern urban homes are made of brick or concrete and many are built in a Western style.

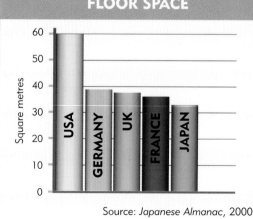

PER CAPITA DWELLING FLOOR SPACE

Source: *Japanese Almanac, 2000*

MIXING TRADITIONAL AND MODERN LIFESTYLES

Japanese homes often reflect a mixture of modern and traditional lifestyles. Even in a modern home, shoes are removed in the hall or entryway and slippers are put on. Separate waterproof slippers are worn in the bathroom, and living rooms will have *tatami* mats (thick straw mats on the floor) on which to sit and *kotatsu* or foot-warmers to keep out the cold in winter. However, other aspects of the Japanese lifestyle are utterly modern, for example many homes have air-conditioning and a vast array of hi-tech gadgets.

Many Japanese people still wear traditional footwear for certain occasions, as well as the latest designer trainers, of course!

Increasing numbers of people now live in detached or semi-detached houses. In the newer developments such as Tama (see page 51) these are attractively laid out, threaded with paths and cycleways, planted with trees and shrubs, and provided with neighbourhood facilities. In some areas cars are separated from the pedestrian routes, providing an air of tranquillity and cleanliness. However, many people in Japan regret the passing of the traditional architecture that was so well adapted to both the hazardous environment and the varied climate. These simple traditional homes tended to be made of wood. They stayed cool in summer, warm in winter and could easily be rebuilt if damaged by floods or earthquakes.

This house has a traditional roof, brought up to date with the latest solar heating panels.

PERSONAL COMPUTERS (PER 1,000 PEOPLE)

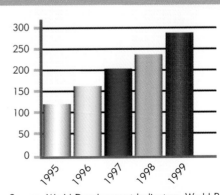

Source: World Development Indicators, World Bank

Tea pickers work to bring in the harvest. Tea is an important crop in Japan.

Japan has very few natural resources. Minerals such as iron ore, copper, zinc, lead and silver, and important energy resources such as oil and coal all have to be imported. The Japanese landscape and climate present farmers with a number of difficulties, and while the country does produce some key crops, such as rice, around half of its food has to be imported from elsewhere.

Planting out young rice seedlings is a crucial time in the farming year.

FARMING

Japan's mountainous slopes are often too steep to cultivate and much of the flat land is now given over to urban or industrial use. The land that lies in between has to be terraced to make it suitable for farming. The country does have plentiful rainfall and most of the islands are warm apart from Hokkaido, but Japan is also prone to typhoons in early autumn and to heavy snowfall in winter. On the coast, the flatlands are at risk from occasional tsunami and some of the mountain areas are subject to volcanic eruptions.

RICE

Despite such difficult conditions, farming is very important to the Japanese economy and the agricultural sector is dominated by the cultivation of rice. Many farms, however, are small. Most farmers (about 78 per cent) work part-time and much of the work is done by women.

PEST CONTROL

Japan's rice cultivation in the past 50 years has involved intensive use of fertilisers, herbicides and pesticides. Their use has had many side effects, notably the pollution of many inland lakes. Recently, there have been attempts to develop alternatives. These include the unusual step of introducing carp to some of the flooded paddy fields to act as natural controls on the pests.

Rice needs particular conditions in which to grow. Seeds are usually cultivated under plastic greenhouses until they become seedlings. The young plants are then planted out with their roots covered by at least 10cm of water. Substantial engineering works are required to provide the irrigation and drainage systems needed for the paddy fields. The rice eventually matures in autumn and turns golden-brown, like wheat, before it is harvested. Rice is grown throughout Japan, even in Hokkaido. Most is grown further south, however, and there are a number of specialist areas such as Niigata.

OTHER CROPS

Although rice is undoubtedly Japan's most important crop, other grains are cultivated, in particular barley to supply the country's massive brewing industry. A wide range of fruit and vegetables, such as tomatoes, cucumbers, sweet potatoes, lettuces, apples and nectarines, is also farmed.

Tea is also grown in Japan, particularly on the terraces on the slopes of the mountains. The main crop produced is the green tea

TIMBER

Japan is rich in woodland but it is not self-sufficient in timber. Much of the woodland lies in remote mountainous areas, which are expensive to exploit. The forests are often in areas of outstanding natural beauty and there are environmental objections to their removal. Another problem is that the types of tree that grow in Japan meet only part of the demand. In particular the Japanese use tropical hardwoods for furniture and arts and crafts. There is also a substantial demand for low-grade timber that can be used to produce wood chips for use in furniture and wood pulp. As a result, Japan has in the past invested in the exploitation of tropical rainforests in South-east Asia, for which it has been criticised by a number of environmental organisations.

LAND RESOURCES (NOT RICE)

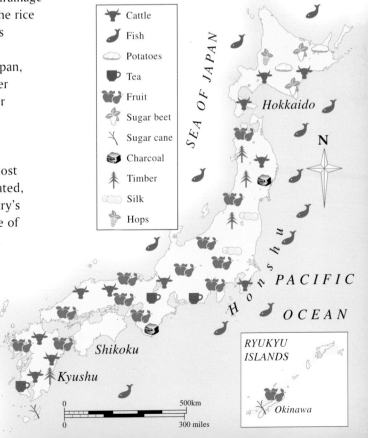

Cattle
Fish
Potatoes
Tea
Fruit
Sugar beet
Sugar cane
Charcoal
Timber
Silk
Hops

SEA OF JAPAN

Hokkaido

N

Honshu

PACIFIC

OCEAN

Shikoku

RYUKYU ISLANDS

EAST CHINA SEA

Kyushu

0   500km
0   300 miles

Okinawa

FISHING

For many years Japan caught more fish than any other country in the world. The Japanese have always consumed large amounts of fish and seafood, as well as other products of the sea such as seaweed. However, like other great fishing nations, Japan has suffered depletion of both its coastal and deep-sea fisheries in recent years.

In terms of per capita consumption of fish and other seafood, Japan is second only to Iceland.

Japan's fish catches have slipped due to depleted fishing stocks in its coastal waters and international restrictions on deep-sea fishing. It is now ranked only third in the world. To compensate for this the country has increased its aquaculture or fish farming industry. It has also increased the volume of

The tuna fish auctions at Tokyo's Tsujuki fish market are a popular tourist attraction – for those willing to be there at 5 a.m.

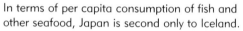
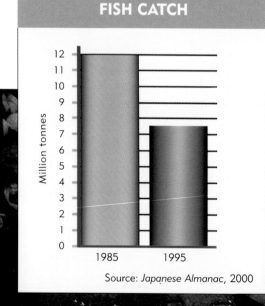

FISH CATCH

Source: *Japanese Almanac*, 2000

its imports, which by 1997 had risen to nearly 6 million tonnes. Fish is still an important part of the Japanese diet and accounts for almost 40 per cent of the population's intake of animal protein, a figure far higher than that of most Western countries.

The decline in the fishing fleet has had a drastic impact on many fishing communities. Employment figures in the industry have declined by nearly half in the past 30 years and now fishing accounts for only around 280,000 jobs. Fishing communities have been hit by a number of problems ranging from environmental protesters to pollution in inland waters. The principal problem was, however, overfishing. This created an unsustainable industry – too many fish were being caught before they had a chance to breed successfully and replace fish stocks. The resulting decline has created pockets of unemployment in some coastal areas.

WHALING

In the past, the whaling industry hunted many whale species to near extinction. In a response to this, the International Whaling Commission (IWC) imposed a ban on whaling in the 1990s. Japan is one of only a minority of nations – others include Iceland and Norway – that wish to resume whaling. Their prime target is the minke whale. The global population of minke probably exceeds 500,000. The Japanese believe that, if properly monitored, the industry could provide a sustainable yield (a catch that would not reduce the breeding population). The Japanese also argue that whale meat is popular in the country and that a number of seafaring communities have come to depend on whaling for their livelihoods.

The moral arguments surrounding this issue are complex and emotive. Environmentalists are concerned that there is still a danger of hunting the minke whale to extinction. They also point out that killing whales with harpoons is particularly cruel. Some environmentalists have suggested that a better alternative would be to employ the whaling fleet to take tourists to view the whales as an example of eco-tourism. In some places this is already happening.

In 2001 the IWC debated the ban again and it was upheld, this time by a reduced majority. The Japanese are allowed to continue to hunt and catch a number of mainly minke whales for scientific research purposes. However, hunting the whales for food is clearly still going on, as whale meat can still be found on the menu in bars in Tokyo and other Japanese ports.

Many of Japan's fishing boats work from picturesque harbours such as this one in Kyushu.

ENERGY RESOURCES

It is astonishing that a country with such limited energy resources as Japan has achieved the industrial might it has today. However, Japan's rapid growth has left it with a major problem – the country has to import over 80 per cent of its fuel. In the case of fossil fuels, this figure is almost 100 per cent.

In the mid-1990s most of Japan's oil imports were from the Middle East. This made Japan very vulnerable to political instability in a volatile part of the world. The government has taken several steps to tackle this problem.

CONSERVING ENERGY

During the 1970s and 1980s, the Japanese government passed legislation to improve the country's energy efficiency. As a result, electricity and oil consumption fell by 15 per cent, though this figure began to creep up again after 1985. This was achieved through energy conservation, particularly in the industrial sector. The iron and steel industry, for example, reduced its energy use per tonne of steel by over a quarter between 1973 and

1987. The Japanese believe they have now reached the limits of cost-effective energy conservation. Japan's per capita energy consumption is less than that of the USA and France, but slightly higher than that of the UK. Despite the conservation measures overall energy demand has continued to grow. This is mainly due to changing lifestyles,

Japan is a highly industrialised country, but it has to import nearly all its oil.

Electricity production is so important that power stations can even be seen near religious sites, such as this one near one of Japan's 'Three Great Scenic Beauties' at Matsushima.

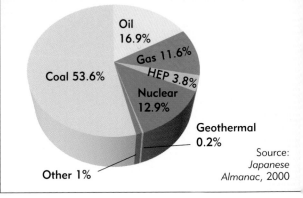

BREAKDOWN OF ENERGY USE

Oil 16.9%
Gas 11.6%
Coal 53.6%
HEP 3.8%
Nuclear 12.9%
Geothermal 0.2%
Other 1%

Source: Japanese Almanac, 2000

including greater use of energy-using devices in homes, such as air-conditioning and home heating, and increased use of private cars. The concern over oil supply also prompted the government to initiate a massive programme of stockpiling. The Japanese government now has oil reserves stored in several centres strategically located across the country.

NUCLEAR POWER AND ALTERNATIVE ENERGY SOURCES

Like other developed nations with limited fossil fuel resources, Japan has become increasingly attracted to nuclear power. In recent years, the government has undertaken an ambitious programme of nuclear power station construction. By 1999, 51 stations had been completed and they now produce over a third of the electricity generated.

Japan has also invested in alternative forms of energy. It has made extensive use of hydro-electric power (HEP). The country also exploits geothermal energy, for example in Beppu and Mount Aso National Park in Kyushu. There has also been investment in solar, tidal, wave, wind and hydrogen power. However, it is likely to be many years before Japan can substantially reduce its need for traditional forms of energy.

CASE STUDY
DANGERS OF NUCLEAR POWER

In 1995 there was an accident at an experimental reactor in Monju when a leak occurred, spraying 1,500 tonnes of reactive material into an equipment room. Although no radioactivity was released to the environment, plant operators were found to have covered up their mistakes and the company was fined by the government. Another accident at a fuel processing plant at Tokaimura in 1997 was more serious. A fire and explosion led to over 35 staff being exposed to a small amount of radiation.

The public has become concerned about the safety of nuclear power stations. Some opinion polls now indicate that 90 per cent of the population feel uneasy about nuclear power. In a referendum held in 1996, citizens of Maki in western Honshu voted against the construction of a nuclear power station in their area. Despite such opposition the government has given the go-ahead to clean up Monju with a view to re-opening it.

Shipbuilding has always been an important industry in Japan.

Japan's industrial development dates back to the nineteenth century. With the opening up of trade that followed the Meiji Restoration in 1868, Japan's industry grew rapidly. By the 1900s, Japan was able to equip substantial military forces from its industrial base in iron and steel, shipbuilding, vehicle manufacturing, aircraft construction and weapons production.

Throughout the early twentieth century Japan expanded. Its armies took over large territories, notably Korea and the Chinese province of Manchuria. Then, on 7 December 1941, Japan attacked the US naval base in Pearl Harbor, Hawaii. The USA joined the Second World War against Japan and Germany. At first the war went well for Japan, but by 1945 its cities were within the range of enemy bombers. Much of Japan's industry was targeted by the Allied bombers, which devastated cities such as Tokyo, Niigata, Osaka, Fukuoka, Hiroshima and Nagasaki. These last two cities were the first ever to be attacked with atomic bombs. In 1945, after defeat in the war, Japanese industrialists began the process of rebuilding their plants.

THE POST-WAR MIRACLE

Japan's fortunes changed when the Korean War broke out in 1950. The USA was keen for Japan to help in the manufacture of weapons for forces supporting South Korea. Industrial output, particularly in sectors such as iron and steel production and shipbuilding, grew rapidly. Thanks to financial help from the USA and Japan's determination to recover, many new factories had been built by the time the Korean War ended in 1953.

In addition to Japan's labour and management skills the country had other advantages. Many of its industrial plants were new, efficient, economic and sited in excellent locations. Large-scale coastal plants were able

The Gengaku Dome in Hiroshima, a chilling reminder of the horror of nuclear weapons, now sits at the heart of a reborn city.

to import materials in bulk from wherever was cheapest. Output and sales in steel soared. Shipbuilding and other industries also flourished. Newer industries such as electronics, electrical goods and vehicle manufacturing began to blossom. These new industries gave birth to some of the world's leading brand names, such as Sony, Panasonic and Honda.

ECONOMIC SLOWDOWN

Japan's economy is currently the second largest in the world, but weaknesses are beginning to show. In recent years, many companies have become bankrupt – over 17,000 in 1998. The debts of major companies have risen and reached 15,182,000 million yen in the late 1990s. Government debt has reached a staggering 600 trillion yen. Some economists believe that many sectors in the economy are overstaffed and that company costs need to be reduced.

Some Japanese academics believe that the era when Japanese culture's traditional values yielded success is nearing its close. They argue that a greater degree of individualism is needed to stimulate new growth in industry. Some large companies are already changing their management practices, moving away from traditional corporate values and rewarding individual performance. This is an example of Western practices influencing those in Japan.

A NEW ERA?

There are technological trends within Japan that may indicate future strengths. Japan is at the cutting edge of medical technology. New digital-control technology and industrial robotics are other areas where Japan has taken a leading role. Entertainment, and its increasing relationship with computing and communications, is a further area where Japan is well placed – Sony is already a major world player.

Japan is a world leader in technological advances. This technician is working on a virtual robot.

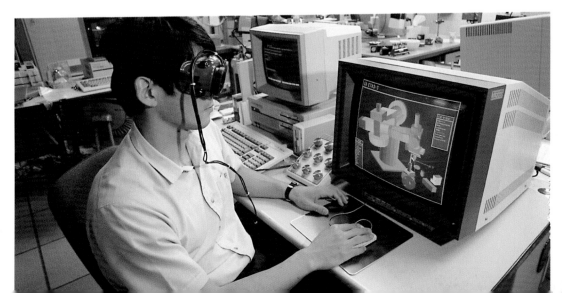

CHANGES IN INDUSTRY

At the turn of the millennium Japanese industry is changing. Japan's early industrial development was based on heavy industry such as iron and steel, chemicals development and shipbuilding. These industries experienced a major revival in the 1950s and 1960s, and they are still important both within Japan and abroad. Since then, new industries in the consumer durable (washing machines and TVs) and hi-tech (computers and advanced electronics) sectors have developed. These industries have grown and merged together with traditional ones to form a huge industrial area, known as the Pacific Belt, stretching from eastern Honshu to eastern Kyushu.

THE PACIFIC BELT

The range of industries in the Pacific Belt is immense. The Keihin region (including Tokyo and Kanagawa) is the most important and accounts for 42 per cent of all Japanese industry. This region has many traditional industries such as petrochemicals, steel and vehicle manufacturing, and is also a centre of publishing, printing and textile production. However, it has many hi-tech industries, many of which cluster around the university in the

Vehicle manufacturing is a long-standing industry in Japan. Much of the work is done by robots.

specially created 'Science City' of Tsukuba, about 60km north-east of Tokyo. Companies located in this area include NEC, Hitachi, Canon, Intel and Sanyo.

The Chukyo region (centred around Nagoya) most famously houses the massive Toyota vehicle plant in Toyota City. It also has major textile industries and is an important area of engineering and electrical machinery production. The Hanshin region includes the cities of Kyoto, Osaka and Kobe and, together with Chukyo, is responsible for a quarter of Japanese production. Traditionally, Hanshin concentrated on craft industries and textiles, but some of these have experienced problems in recent years, notably the silk industry. Engineering, petrochemicals, publishing and printing are also important industries in Hanshin.

Kita-Kyushu and Fukuoka are part of an old industrial area of heavy industries based originally on local coalfields. This area is located on the coast, which means that raw materials can be imported easily by ship. Although Kita-Kyushu and Fukuoka only

Japan's mobile phone industry is huge. Most Japanese people have a mobile phone.

account for 2.6 per cent of Japan's manufacturing output, their iron and steel, shipbuilding and petrochemical industries are still significant. This area does, however, need to attract more modern industry if it is to remain important.

NEW DEVELOPMENTS

Recently some new industrial areas have begun to emerge. Much of Kyushu has become a focus of the electronics industry. The area is attractive not only to companies within Japan but also to foreign investors from places such as the USA and Europe.

Other areas that have seen recent growth include southern Hokkaido and the coastal strip alongside the Inland Sea, which links Hiroshima, Okayama and Niihama. To the east of Keihin is another growing zone that incorporates Sendai and Hitachi, and across the Japanese Alps is a developing area linking Fukui and Niigata. These locations all have industries dating back to the early twentieth century but more recently they have blossomed, with the expansion of newer industries producing electrical goods, electronics and computers.

This growing spread of industry looks set to continue, as businesses become freer to set up in a greater range of locations. This would happen more quickly if road and rail systems in the more remote areas of the country were improved. Already the development of the Internet and e-commerce is allowing some small businesses to locate almost anywhere they choose.

THE PACIFIC BELT

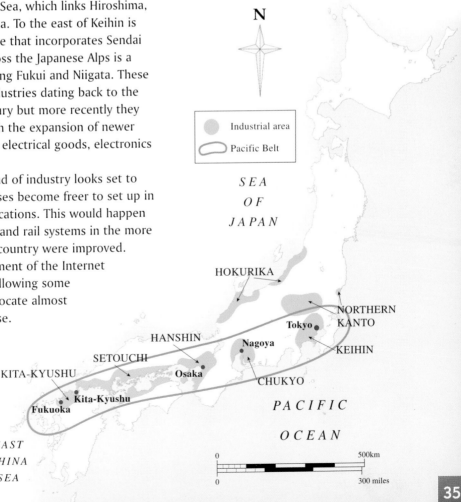

N

Industrial area
Pacific Belt

SEA
OF
JAPAN

HOKURIKA

NORTHERN KANTO

Tokyo

KEIHIN

HANSHIN

Nagoya

SETOUCHI

KITA-KYUSHU

Osaka

CHUKYO

Kita-Kyushu

Fukuoka

PACIFIC

OCEAN

EAST
CHINA
SEA

0   500km

0   300 miles

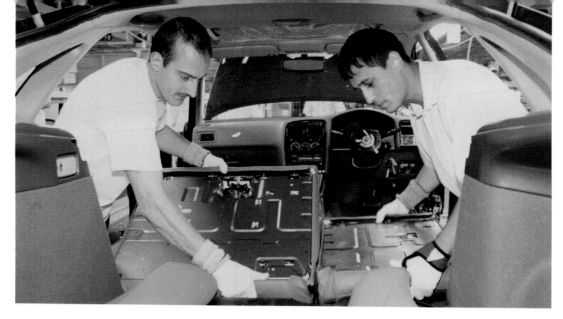

Japanese overseas investment creates new jobs. These two men are working in a Toyota factory in Burnaston, near Derby in the UK.

OVERSEAS INVESTMENT

Japan has become one of the world's largest overseas investors, setting up companies all over the globe. The volume of Japan's overseas assets is colossal. In 1998, they were valued at 133.3 trillion yen. In 1998 alone the country invested 5,216,900 million yen abroad. All types of Japanese companies have invested overseas, with the majority being in the service and property sectors. North America received 26.9 per cent of Japan's overseas investment in 1998 and Europe received 34.4 per cent. Asia has seen a decline in recent years. This represents a shift of investment towards more economically developed countries.

WHY INVEST OVERSEAS?

There are a number reasons for Japanese investment in other countries:

- To get around trade restrictions against foreign goods by manufacturing them where they will be sold, instead of in Japan.

- To make sure that some factories are in areas that are safe from earthquakes.

- To use cheap labour in poorer countries, instead of paying high Japanese wages.

- To be able to use raw materials such as bauxite (used in the production of aluminium).

Japanese investment abroad often has a positive impact on the countries that receive it, such as the creation of jobs. In the UK alone it is estimated that Japanese investment had created 60,000 jobs by the mid-1990s.

Japanese multinational companies such as Sony have invested worldwide. This plant is in Basingstoke, in the UK.

OVERSEAS INVESTMENT BY SECTOR

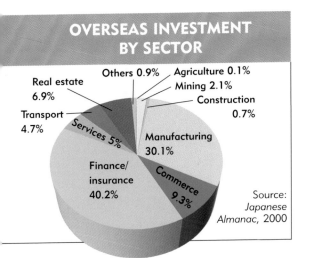

Others 0.9%
Agriculture 0.1%
Mining 2.1%
Construction 0.7%
Real estate 6.9%
Transport 4.7%
Services 5%
Manufacturing 30.1%
Finance/insurance 40.2%
Commerce 9.3%

Source: *Japanese Almanac, 2000*

These have included developments such as Toyota in Burnaston, Nissan in Sunderland and Honda in Swindon. There is a downside to this in that foreign-owned plants are often vulnerable to problems such as worldwide recession. When these factories have to close down, many jobs go with them.

INVESTMENT FROM ABROAD

Investment by foreign companies in Japan is often of major importance. Japan is an attractive place for overseas companies to invest: it is the world's second largest economy, a major industrial innovator and a highly developed country offshore of some of the world's largest potential markets. The investment has tended to focus on manufacturing, but in recent years there has also been some growth in the service sector. In 2000, overseas investment in Japan reached a new high, partly because the value of the yen had dropped in recent years, making it possible to rent offices and employ staff more cheaply. Some people also believe that the long Japanese recession will soon end. More significantly, increased investment probably reflects the success of investment in the country in the past. US and European companies have recently invested large amounts of money in Japan.

CASE STUDY
TEXAS INSTRUMENTS

One of many US companies set up in Japan is the Texas Instruments plant, on the outskirts of Beppu in Kyushu. With good access to air transport at nearby Oita airport, a highly skilled workforce and a clean water supply, the site was an ideal location for the company. The factory, constructed in 1973, is situated on a hill at Hiji overlooking Beppu Bay, where there is a mild climate throughout the year.

The US-owned factory employs 1,300 people in the area. It is environmentally friendly, recycling all its liquids and discharging none to the environment other than the rainwater from its roof. The factory makes digital signal processors that are used in a variety of electronic products such as mobile phones and video recorders. Its production areas are largely controlled by robots.

The Texas Instruments plant in Kyushu.

Small-scale rice farmers now face competition from abroad, with fewer government subsidies.

TRADE

Japan is one of the great global traders. The growth in its overseas trade since 1945 has been remarkable and in 1998 this was valued at 51 billion yen. Japan now earns more in exports than it spends on imports. This gap is known as a trade surplus, which in 1998 was valued at 13,991 billion yen. This imbalance has been a concern for a number of countries which believe Japan has created barriers to exports from other countries. In recent years much pressure has been applied to the Japanese government to allow more foreign goods into the country. There has been some progress in this area, for example government financial support for farmers has declined over the past 20 years. This means that foreign rice farmers are now more likely to be able to sell their crops in Japan.

Over the last 50 years the nature of Japanese trading has changed. In terms of imports, foodstuffs and raw materials have decreased whilst fuel and manufactured goods have increased. Crude oil imports alone were worth about US$20 million in 1998.

Exports such as textiles, chemicals and refined metals have declined whilst machinery and equipment have increased dramatically. Much of this growth is in the vehicle and electronics sectors, where Japan is a world leader.

The geographical pattern of trading has also altered. The volume of imports from the USA and European countries has declined whilst the LEDCs and Asian tigers (Singapore, Thailand, Taiwan and Malaysia) have exported more of their products to Japan. The balance of exports has also changed, almost in the opposite direction. Exports to Asia have declined whilst those to the USA and Europe have greatly increased. This reflects the nature of the products involved. It is more cost-effective for Japan to buy certain products from poorer countries, where labour costs are low and goods can be produced cheaply. However, Japan can sell more of its higher-value consumer items such as electronics to wealthier nations where people have greater disposable incomes.

Japanese companies have used the massive trade surplus to invest a lot of money abroad, buying real estate and foreign companies, and setting up overseas plants. The country has also become the largest aid donor in the world.

Aid

In 1998 Japan donated US$10,683 million in aid, much more than France, Germany and the UK. The distribution of this aid is overwhelmingly to Asia – about 43.3 per cent in 1998, though this is less than in former years. In the past 20 years the top ten recipients of Japanese aid were all Asian countries and included Indonesia, China, the Philippines and Bangladesh. The bulk of Japan's aid has been in the form of loans and grants. Around 50 per cent has been given to support projects such as transport, energy and telecommunications. About a sixth has gone into economic production and slightly less into social

A Japanese aid worker gives some advice to rice farmers in Zambia.

infrastructure (education and health). Whilst Japan has undoubtedly been a major aid donor, it has been criticised for its emphasis on economically oriented projects. Some people argue that Japan should switch this emphasis to more humanitarian aid and fund this directly rather than through loans, which have to be paid back. However, these criticisms tend to come from fellow developed countries rather than the recipients, many of whom have been happy to see the focus on economic progress.

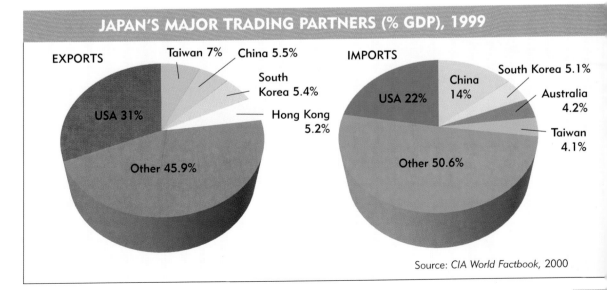

JAPAN'S MAJOR TRADING PARTNERS (% GDP), 1999

EXPORTS

Taiwan 7% China 5.5%
South Korea 5.4%
Hong Kong 5.2%
USA 31%
Other 45.9%

IMPORTS

China 14% South Korea 5.1%
Australia 4.2%
USA 22%
Taiwan 4.1%
Other 50.6%

Source: *CIA World Factbook, 2000*

SERVICES

Japan has seen a massive growth in employment in the retail and service industries. At the same time, numbers of people working in manufacturing and agriculture have declined. In part, this shift in the labour force is due to advances in technology. On farms and in factories, sophisticated machinery and robots now carry out repetitive, menial or dangerous jobs quickly and efficiently, meaning fewer workers are needed to perform such tasks. Changing lifestyles and the migration of people from rural areas to the cities have led to the creation of new types of job, particularly in the financial and banking sectors. The growth in urbanisation has also led to increasing demand for support services such as transport, communications and utilities, and there has been a massive growth in the leisure and tourism industry.

This trend is very similar to that of Western economies, but in Japan there are some marked differences. The service sector that sells directly to the public in shops, banks, restaurants and entertainment is more heavily staffed than in other countries such as the USA or the UK. The number of staff employed in filling stations is a good example of this.

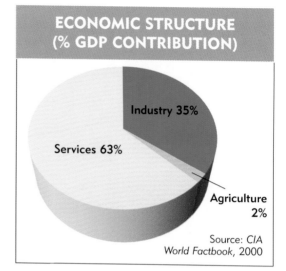

ECONOMIC STRUCTURE (% GDP CONTRIBUTION)

Industry 35%

Services 63%

Agriculture 2%

Source: CIA World Factbook, 2000

Rather than providing self-service facilities, almost all garages employ someone to serve customers with petrol. Whilst this is underway a second person will clean the windscreen, while another checks the oil level. Another place where high staffing levels can be seen is the *shinkansen* or bullet train service. When one of these trains draws into Tokyo station a whole team of staff are lined up along the platform at every carriage, ready to clean the train before it departs. Large numbers of staff are also employed to clean streets, not only in the city centres but also in the residential streets of new developments. As well as making Japan a very clean place to live, the service sector also helps to keep people in employment – Japan's unemployment figures are well below that of many Western nations despite the recession.

SHOPPING

The high number of people employed in services is a reflection of Japan's consumer society. The Japanese love to shop; in fact, shopping has been described as the country's modern religion. On Sundays many high streets are closed to cars, to enable the hordes of shoppers to move with at least some degree of freedom. However, progress through a shopping centre at Sunday lunchtime can be a slow business.

A cleaning team lines up to work on the next *shinkansen* when it arrives in Tokyo station.

This obsession with shopping results from Japan's increased affluence – as the country became richer, people had more money to spend. In the 1960s, the 'three sacred treasures' (the things that everyone wanted to own) of the average household were the washing machine, the refrigerator and the TV. In the 1980s and early 1990s these gave way to the car, air-conditioning and the colour TV. Other goods such as pianos, Western-style beds, cameras and advanced electronic goods are now popular, and most households own a mobile phone and laptop computer. Although traditional clothes such as the kimono have recently become popular again, most Japanese now wear Western clothes, at least outside the home. There is competition to buy the latest Western designer labels, despite the high cost of these garments.

A vast range of specialist shops and huge luxury department stores have grown up to meet the demands of Japanese consumers. Outside the modern shopping malls, however, there are still many traditional shops. These can be very specialised and range from cycle repair stores to shops selling dried fish products. There are also local markets selling a wide range of products, many of them local farm produce; street traders selling their home-grown vegetables; and mobile fruit and vegetable merchants selling their goods from the rear of small vans.

The busy shopping mall in Oita.

TELEVISION SETS PER 1,000 HOUSEHOLDS

Source: ITU (International Telecommunications Union)

A street vendor sells some of his produce from the back of his truck.

THE LEISURE INDUSTRY

Although the Japanese work long hours, there is a major leisure and tourism industry. Much leisure time is focused on corporate activity, with many men in particular socialising after work with their colleagues. Young women in work are often affluent and have plenty of money to spend on travel and other activities.

In many ways Japan's leisure pursuits differ little from those of Western countries. The most popular activities are eating out, travelling around the country, *karaoke*, watching videos and listening to music – only *karaoke* is especially Japanese and that has now become popular in other countries around the world.

Many Japanese spend their leisure time on day trips to theme parks such as Disneyland Tokyo or visits to national parks.

In terms of sport, sumo wrestling is traditional but baseball and golf have grown in popularity. Young people today are also keen on football and Japan played host to the World Cup jointly with South Korea in 2002.

More traditional entertainment with *geisha* is less common but still exists, especially in Kyoto and Tokyo. The *geisha* are professional entertainers who undergo a long period

PACHINKO

One craze that has become popular in Japan is *pachinko*, a simple form of pinball. *Pachinko* parlours have grown up on a massive scale in recent years. Some are tucked away in city areas, but the number of out-of-town parlours is increasing. These are neon-lit palaces occupying large sites with extensive car parks. The games are relatively cheap to play and require little effort, a factor that probably contributes to their popularity.

A *pachinko* parlour in outer Tokyo.

LEFT: Recently, interest in the traditional kimono has been revived among young women.
BELOW: Football is becoming a popular sport among the young in Japan.

CASE STUDY
'WELCOME PLAN 21'

In 2001, the Japanese government conducted an extensive survey into tourist attitudes to Japan. Questions covered subjects such as fears of natural disasters, language difficulties, travel problems and immigration. The country is implementing 'Welcome Plan 21', designed to boost foreign visitor numbers to 8 million by 2004. A number of actions have already been taken such as providing information on trains in English, although this does not yet apply to all suburban routes and some routes outside Tokyo. In addition to this telephone lines have been set up in the major cities to ensure that tourists and information centres can always find at least one member of staff who can speak English. Japan has much to offer in terms of its natural landscapes and cultural heritage, and the Japanese are undoubtedly some of the most polite, helpful and hospitable people on the planet.

of training in the arts of conversation, dance, etiquette and playing a traditional stringed instrument called the *shamisen*. A night out with a *geisha* is expensive. Working as a *geisha* appears to be becoming more popular again with young women.

TOURISM

The Japanese are among the most-travelled people in the world, spending much of their disposable income on foreign holidays. However, the tourist industry within Japan attracts relatively few visitors from abroad. In 1999, 16.4 million Japanese travelled abroad but only 4.4 million tourists visited Japan. The country ranks only 35th in the world in terms of inbound tourism, below many of its South-east Asian neighbours such as Singapore and Malaysia. At present most visitors to Japan come from Taiwan, South Korea, the USA and the UK. Even so, the number of Japanese people visiting the UK heavily outweighs those arriving in Japan from the UK. The top eight holiday destinations for the Japanese are the USA, South Korea, Hong Kong, China, Taiwan, Australia, Thailand and Singapore.

CASE STUDY
MAJOR NATIONAL PARKS

1. Shikotsu-Toya
2. Shiretoko
3. Akan
4. Kushiro-Shitsugen
5. Daisetsuzan
6. Bandai-Asahi
7. Nikko
8. Fuji-Hakone-Izu
9. Yoshino-Kumano
10. Ise-Shima
11. Unzen-Amakusa
12. Aso-Kuju
13. Daisen-Oki
14. Hakusan
15. Chubu Sangaku
16. Minami-Alps
17. Chichibu-Tama
18. Towada-Hachimantai

SEA OF JAPAN

PACIFIC OCEAN

EAST CHINA SEA

500km
300 miles

The Japanese have a great reverence for nature. The essence of the Shinto religion is 'harmony with nature', so it is not surprising that visits to the countryside are a favourite Japanese leisure activity. Over 30 million people visited the country's national parks in 1997. The national parks date back to the 1930s and cover about 5.4 per cent of Japan's land area. They include some of the country's most spectacular scenery.

The most famous national park is probably Fuji-Hakone-Izu, which includes Japan's best-known mountain feature, the dormant volcano Mount Fuji. The park can easily be reached from some of Japan's largest cities, Tokyo, Yokohama and Nagoya, and attracts over 10 million tourists each year.

Japanese taxi doors open automatically and the seats are immaculate.

The physical landscape of Japan, combined with its many natural hazards, offers a considerable challenge to the development of communications networks. Despite this the Japanese have invested heavily in improvements to their transport infrastructure. The best known of the country's transport systems is its high-speed rail network, known as the *shinkansen* or bullet train network.

In preparation for the Tokyo Olympics in 1964, the government felt it needed a modern express rail system. New railway lines were designed to follow more direct routes across the country and high-speed trains were developed using the most advanced technology of the day. These combined to increase speeds, punctuality, reliability and comfort. The *shinkansen* is still one of the fastest trains in the world, overtaken only by the French TGV.

There has also been considerable investment in non-*shinkansen* expresses such as the Sonic tilting train that connects Hakata with Oita along the winding lines of eastern Kyushu. Urban transport systems have also been improved. The various cities have many different transport systems – trams in Okayama and Hiroshima, subways in Kyoto and monorails in Kita-Kyushu.

Tokyo has a massive array of commuter lines, subways and buses. In addition to this is a massive fleet of taxis, all of which have white-lined seats and automated opening and shutting of the rear doors.

Although car ownership has grown rapidly, it has been difficult to develop the road system and expressways are still relatively limited, especially away from the Tokaido Megalopolis.

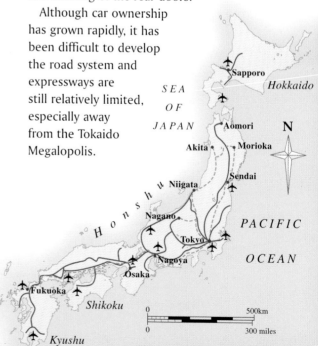

— Expressways
----- *Shinkansen* lines
✈ Airports

A train manager keeps an eye on the platform to make sure passengers board safely.

Japan had a dense network of railways that dated back to the nineteenth century, but it was relatively slow due to the mountainous terrain. With the coming of the Tokyo Olympics in 1964, the government felt that the country needed a new express system. The first *shinkansen* line was the Tokaido line, built to link Tokyo with Shin Osaka. This was extended to Hakata in Kyushu. Tokyo was then linked to Morioka (later extended to Akita) and to Niigata. The new system meant much shorter journey times – two and a half hours from Tokyo to Shin Osaka at speeds of up to 270 kilometres per hour with 11 trains an hour in each direction. The service has proved very popular with passengers. Trains have been continuously upgraded and some of the recent carriages look more like airline cabins than traditional trains, with computer consoles and power-point facilities on board. New developments are underway to extend the system further but these are major building projects and will take many years to complete.

Expressways are toll roads and they are expensive to use. Freight movements by road have increased massively but large trucks and lorries tend to avoid the tolls and so the ordinary trunk roads are often congested and traffic jams are common.

Japan also has a major international network of air routes based around the national airline, Japan Airlines (JAL). The airline has an extensive fleet of planes and operates many long-distance routes, for example, the non-stop flights from Tokyo and Osaka to London Heathrow or Paris. Marine transport is also important internationally and internally between the islands.

In terms of telecommunications Japan is very advanced. Mobile phone use is at a high level, particularly amongst the young. Many now connect computers to mobile phones and it is a common sight on the *shinkansen* to see executives checking their e-mail.

Overall, Japan has a very sophisticated transport and communications infrastructure. Public transport is plentiful, effective and efficient. Further developments such as the magnetic-levitation high-speed train, new island-linking bridges and more expressways should provide further freedom of movement.

A monorail glides smoothly above the streets in Chiba.

TELECOMMUNICATIONS DATA

Mainline Phones	60,300,000
Mobile Phones	36,500,000
Internet Service Providers	357

Source: *CIA World Factbook*

Crowds of people hurry to work in the city during the rush hour.

Most people in Japan live in towns and cities. The massive urban complex that stretches from Tokyo through to Kobe is home to one of the most extensive built-up areas in the world. This area is known as the Tokaido Megalopolis.

Although most of the Tokaido Megalopolis only dates back to 1945, cities and towns in Japan have a long history. Many of the present cities originated or expanded as military towns during shogun rule. They tended to be sited at crossroads where rivers or other routeways converged. Most were located in Japan's lowlands, particularly in the Kanto and Kansai plains. Many grew very quickly. For example, in 1590 Edo (now called Tokyo) was a collection of fishing villages. By 1690 it housed a million people and was probably the largest city in the world.

At the same time Kyoto, the imperial capital, had a population of 600,000 and in Osaka the figure was almost as high. A number of provincial cities such as Nagoya had populations of over 50,000. By 1878 Japan had 99 towns and cities, and these were home to 10 per cent of the population. This made Japan the most urbanised nation in the pre-industrial world.

RAPID URBANISATION

The Meiji government stimulated population growth, agricultural reform and industrialisation. These measures encouraged more people to move from the countryside to urban areas – there were 230 of these by 1920, although most of the growth was in just four areas:

- Tokyo-Yokohama;
- Osaka-Kyoto-Kobe;
- Nagoya;
- Fukuoka-Kita-Kyushu.

A quarter of the population now lived in towns – urban areas were booming as communities grew and people started families. By contrast, rural areas, particularly those in the mountains, suffered economic and social decline. There an ageing society began to emerge.

Since 1920 the urban population in Japan has mushroomed, as more and more people have migrated from rural areas to the cities. Growth was particularly fast up to 1960, although it has eased since then. Indeed some people have

Land has to be reclaimed in Japan to create space on which to build new urban developments.

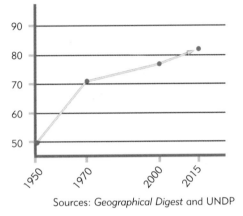

URBAN POPULATION (% OF TOTAL)

Sources: *Geographical Digest* and UNDP

begun to move out. This has happened because of the high cost of housing, improved transport links, the availability of better quality housing in the suburbs and encouragement from local governments.

Today, however, three great metropolitan areas continue to dominate the urban landscape. Tokyo alone has 24 per cent of the total population, Osaka 13 per cent and Nagoya 7 per cent. This leaves only 56 per cent in the rest of the country.

Tokyo is overwhelmingly dominant and is what geographers call a primate city – it is over twice the size of the second largest city and it has a stranglehold on functions such as government, culture, education, the media, big business, shopping and entertainment. However, having so many important functions centred in one place is dangerous. If Tokyo were hit by a major earthquake, the destruction could be crippling.

Japan's rapid urbanisation created a number of problems: cramped housing conditions, intense competition for land and spiralling property prices. It has also contributed to a lack of structure – most of the cities appear rather chaotic, with none of the separation of housing from industry and commerce that is seen in many other developed countries.

There is no shortage of land in the countryside, but it is often too mountainous to build on.

Tokyo's main station is at the heart of the country's *shinkansen* network.

TOKYO

Tokyo was founded as Edo by the shogun leader, Tokugawa Ieyasu, in 1598. The city's origins lie in a small fishing community, with access to a natural deepwater, sheltered harbour. Edo was also a route centre in Japan's most extensive area of flat land, the Kanto Plain. The army built a castle in Edo and the city gradually emerged as a centre of local government, religion, culture and commerce.

The lights of downtown Tokyo shine all night long.

TOKYO'S DEVELOPMENT

In the 1860s, the Meiji government decided to move Japan's capital from Kyoto to Edo. The city was renamed Tokyo, meaning 'eastern capital' and so began its modern growth. One of the first developments was the construction of the Imperial Palace in Akasaka. Close by the *Diet* (Japanese parliament), the ministries and Supreme Court were built. These attracted financial institutions such as the *Bourse* (Stock Exchange), Bank of Japan and numerous company headquarters to the area. The government also set up important educational and cultural establishments in the city. The Imperial University (now the University of Tokyo), a number of theatres, and shopping and entertainment districts soon followed.

Tokyo's port and links to the rich agricultural region of the Kanto Plain made it attractive to industry. Initially many of the industries were associated with processing agricultural, forest and fish products. Food, paper, cardboard and textile industries emerged later. The increasing range of imports stimulated the development of chemical and iron and steel plants. The products of each of these industries in turn generated further manufacturing in sectors such as engineering, shipbuilding and transport construction. This combination of administrative, commercial and manufacturing activities created plenty of job opportunities, attracting many newcomers to the city. Tokyo's population had reached 3 million by 1920.

WHEN DISASTER STRUCK...

In 1923, the Great Kanto earthquake tore through Tokyo. The destruction was devastating: 104,000 people were killed and 52,000 injured; 63 per cent of the buildings were lost and a further 10 per cent damaged. The losses ran to several billion yen. By 1940 the city had been rebuilt. However, only a few years later further destruction followed. During the Second World War, the Allies subjected Tokyo and most other Japanese cities to a series of fire-bombing raids.

Over 100,000 were killed in Tokyo and, in one raid alone, over 276,000 buildings were destroyed, along with the 70,000 people who inhabited them. The city lay in ruins.

RECOVERY

Tokyo's recovery since 1945 has been remarkable, although it has been at considerable cost to the environment – Tokyo is not a beautiful city. Recent growth is based partly on the city's traditional strengths, which include its activities as a capital and its manufacturing industries. Since 1945 Tokyo has also become an increasingly international city. Japanese company headquarters have become the headquarters of transnational corporations (TNCs). Foreign companies often open their Japanese headquarters in Tokyo. Tokyo is one of the world's biggest cities with a population of over 12 million. Living in such a densely populated city does have its drawbacks. Tokyo is massively congested and its urban sprawl continues to invade the countryside beyond. This has led to long journeys to work for commuters and famously overcrowded trains.

The Tokyo Metropolitan Government's Twin Towers were designed by respected architect, Tange Kenzo. The project was heavily criticised for its expense.

With such a lack of space in urban areas, many corporate buildings make use of their roofs. This building has a helipad on top.

URBAN PROBLEMS OF TOKYO

It is hardly surprising that a city the size of Tokyo has many problems. These include a poor environment, low-quality housing and traffic congestion. Planners have attempted to tackle these problems in a variety of ways. Early projects focused on limiting the spread of the city with a green belt policy, but development pressures were too great for this to succeed and the policy was abandoned.

DECENTRALISATION

In the late 1960s a policy of decentralisation was put forward. This meant encouraging new construction and business to locate away from the city centre. One such scheme involved a group of developments along the Yamanote railway line, which forms a loop around central Tokyo and intersects most of the commuter lines and subways coming from the suburbs. These transport interchanges make good places for businesses to site. They include Shinjuku, Ikebukuro and the

Waterfront Centre. Many of these developments have been successful, and although they have not reduced central congestion, they have at least prevented it from getting worse.

A later scheme proposed new centres of employment and services further from Tokyo. These included a new town at Tama, in the Tama Hills to the west of the capital.

A NEW CAPITAL CITY?

Tokyo dominates the national economy. The city still attracts a huge amount of investment and the population is growing. Many people have questioned whether this dominance is healthy for the nation as a whole, particularly as Tokyo experiences a major earthquake every 70 or so years. The last major tremor was in 1923 so another one could happen at any time.

The potential effects of a large earthquake are almost unimaginable. Since the Great Kanto earthquake Tokyo has grown both upward and outward. It has also become one of the major financial centres of the world. Apart from the potential loss of life and property there could be other effects that would be felt worldwide if a major earthquake hit the city. One economist has suggested that such destruction in the capital would involve a crash of the yen and a global recession as Japan sold off its overseas assets to pay for a rebuilding programme.

In the Tama Hills, to the west of Tokyo lies Tama, a new town that was intended to act as an 'overspill' for Tokyo city centre and as a community in its own right. Construction began in 1965 and is due for completion by 2010.

The town centre has been built around commuter lines to central Tokyo. It is pedestrianised and has department stores, a large supermarket and local shops, along with a cluster of offices and financial services. Housing is grouped in distinctive zones and includes a range of townhouses, mid-rise apartments and detached houses. The neighbourhoods are separated by greenery and recreation spaces. The town is very clean and provides a more spacious and pleasant environment than much of Tokyo. It also provides affordable housing. However, as a self-sustaining centre that is independent of the capital, it has been less successful. For many it has become a dormitory town, a place where people live but commute to work in downtown Tokyo.

Tama's housing districts have clean, spacious walkways and offer a pleasant environment for residents.

Another concern is that too much economic and other investment is concentrated in Tokyo and should be spread more widely across Japan. Some people believe that government should be physically separate from business, as it is in Brazil, for example. If the government moves away then land will become available that could allow more commercial development. This would have the additional benefit of boosting the construction industry. There has been much speculation about how decentralisation of the government could be achieved. One idea is the creation of a 'back-up capital' to cope with emergencies. A more radical solution argues for the spread of government functions throughout the regional capitals of Japan. The favourite solution, however, is to relocate the capital.

The Japanese *Diet* in Tokyo. It has been suggested that the government should move to a different city.

CHALLENGES FOR THE FUTURE

A homeless man sleeps rough on the street.

For much of the post-war period, job security was a key feature of Japanese society. Although unemployment figures fluctuated gently upwards from 1960 to 1990, for most of those years job vacancies outnumbered the unemployed. As late as 1990 there were four vacancies for every three people looking for work. More recently, however, this pattern has changed.

During the late 1980s, people working for large corporations experienced exceptional job security. The relationships between staff and employer were good. Employers provided salaries that rose with age and a range of other benefits such as pensions and medical care. Staff, in turn, were loyal, cooperative and hard-working. This created a high level of productivity that enabled Japan to be competitive with other economies where labour costs were lower. It was an era of great optimism.

The 1990s, however, saw a sustained economic downturn. Gross National Product (GNP) fell into decline in 1996 and has not yet recovered. By contrast, bankruptcies and corporate debt have risen. This has forced companies to cut costs. Shedding labour has not been a traditional Japanese response to economic difficulty. Faced with such problems, however, a reduction in the workforce was seen as inevitable.

THE IMPACT OF UNEMPLOYMENT

Unemployment has almost doubled since 1990. The figure is still low by Western standards but high by those of Japan. This rise in unemployment levels has had some serious effects. Suicide rates have risen significantly. Social security expenditure increased from 11,614,800 million yen in 1990 to 16,095,000 million yen in 1999. Criminal offences also rose dramatically from 1,637,000 in 1990 to 2,034,000 in 1998.

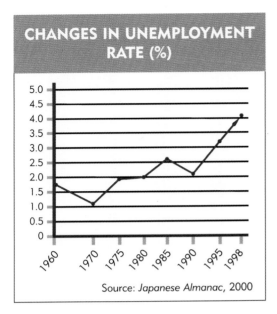

CHANGES IN UNEMPLOYMENT RATE (%)

Source: *Japanese Almanac*, 2000

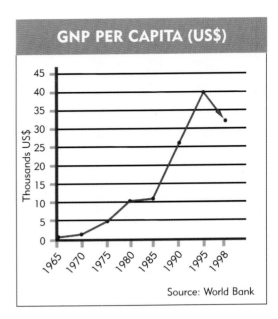

GNP PER CAPITA (US$)

Source: World Bank

These are, of course, selective statistics and do not tell the whole story. By contrast, the number of people killed in gun-related incidents has almost halved in the same time.

Even so, there is an impression of growing social problems that are probably related, at least in part, to unemployment and increasing insecurity.

CASE STUDY
FROM BOOM TO BUST

Hibaya Park in Tokyo is one of many refuges for those down on their luck.

Unemployment has had a catastrophic effect on some people in Japan. In a society where having a useful role is important and unemployment has been rare, some men fail to tell their families of their fate. To retain their sense of honour, they continue to leave for work each morning and return in the evening, until their savings run out and they are forced to explain their situation to their partners. Others have joined 'down and outs' in areas such as Airin in downtown Osaka, where they rely on food handouts from charitable organisations. Some sleep on the streets or in parks in cities such as Tokyo. In Hibaya Park near Tokyo station, for example, there is a significant homeless community. Other places of refuge include the bridges of Kyoto, and stations and subways in all the major cities. Whilst some of these unfortunate people have little more than a plastic bag of basic possessions, some live in temporary homes that contain significant amounts of personal belongings – a few are even connected into electricity supplies.

For some people it is all too much. The loss of livelihood and prospects combined with the loss of honour can lead to alcoholism, or even suicide.

ENVIRONMENTAL PROBLEMS

Japan's environmental problems are rooted in its post-war economic success. During the economic boom in the 1950s and 1960s energy consumption rose dramatically. Combined with other industrial and agricultural practices, this contributed to an increase in pollution.

POLLUTION

Air pollution has grown as a result of high industrial emissions, home heating and increased car use. Japan's sulphur dioxide and nitrogen dioxide emissions more than trebled in the 1960s. Since then sulphur dioxide levels have fallen, but nitrogen dioxide and smoke particulate levels have remained high, and many of Japan's cities have been affected by acid rain and smog.

Water pollution also became a serious problem as a result of growing amounts of effluent (sewage and waste) from homes and factories. Increasing nitrate and pesticide pollution from agriculture has also affected many water bodies.

WASTE DISPOSAL

The disposal of domestic and industrial waste has become a big problem. In 1996, the volume of domestic waste reached 152,000 tonnes a day. Around 66 per cent of this waste was incinerated and much of the rest was disposed of in landfill sites, many of them on land reclaimed from the sea. Industrial waste reached 405 million tonnes a year in 1996, of which 37 per cent was recycled. Some of these wastes have led to serious pollution incidents such as mercury poisoning.

POLLUTION SOLUTION?

The pollution problems of the 1950s and 1960s led to a public outcry that prompted the government to establish one of the most effective anti-pollution programmes in the world. In 1970 the *Diet* (parliament) passed a number of laws that included penalties for individuals or corporations who polluted the environment. In May 1971 the Environment Agency was established, and for the first time

Bags of rubbish await collection on Tokyo's streets. Domestic waste is a huge problem here.

Heavy industry pumps dangerous emissions into the atmosphere.

Face masks can protect wearers from inhaling dust and fumes.

the government showed a genuine willingness to counteract pollution, even at the risk of limiting economic growth. Japan's new emission standards were among the strictest in the world. The 'Polluter Pays' principle was introduced, whereby polluters were charged for their emissions and for the illnesses caused by them.

ENVIRONMENTAL PROTECTION AND CONSERVATION

Problems remain, however, in the areas of environmental protection and nature conservation. Agricultural productivity still relies heavily on the use of herbicides and pesticides. Only 853km^2 of Japan are designated as wildlife protection areas and the country has been one of the world's largest traders in endangered species.

Japan's approach to environmental problems has tended to focus on the prevention of harm to human health rather than the protection of the natural environment or the prevention of pollution in the first place. Whilst the country has been successful in establishing technological solutions, it has been less so in changing social attitudes, such as reducing car use or modifying the 'throw-away society'. More emphasis is needed on the development of manufacturing processes which produce fewer pollutants and that recycle their wastes. This is happening in many major firms but the practice needs to become more widespread.

CASE STUDY
KYOTO CONFERENCE

In December 1997, Japan hosted the Kyoto Conference on Climate Change. As its contribution to the Kyoto agreement Japan introduced a bill to reduce all six greenhouse gases. In 1996 Japan discharged 2.5 tonnes of CO_2 per capita into the environment, placing the country seventh in world rankings, behind the USA, Germany and the UK – the US figure at 5.4 tonnes is more than double that of Japan. The Japanese therefore feel that they have done more than many countries in improving their energy efficiency and reducing the emission of harmful gases, and that the country is disadvantaged by some of the Kyoto proposals. Japan is particularly concerned not to lose ground to the USA, which pulled out of the Kyoto agreement in 2001. Despite some difficult negotiations in 2001, Japan did agree to sign up to a modified treaty.

THE CHANGING ROLE OF WOMEN

To many Westerners the role of women in Japanese society appears rather old-fashioned. The world's media still portray an image of women tied to the home whilst their husbands go to work. This image still prevails in many parts of Japanese society. However, the traditional role of women is changing.

Japanese women today are often educated to the same standard as men. Increasing numbers of women have careers or jobs. Young women are particularly affluent and have high disposable incomes. In fact, much of Japanese advertising is aimed at this group of the population.

MARRIAGE AND DIVORCE

Whilst most Japanese women still do get married, they are delaying the age at which they do so. Since 1920 the average age of marriage for women has risen from 21 years to 25 years. Once married, they are also waiting longer to have children. The first child is often the only one and a growth in childcare opportunities has enabled increasing numbers of women to continue in employment.

Another aspect of change is the growing divorce rate. Whilst this is still low by

HOUSEHOLD CHORES

Within the home, the sharing of domestic responsibilities has been slow to change. A recent survey showed that most men were still reluctant to participate in child rearing and the household chores. The authors of the report had expected the willingness of men to help in the home to be dependent on the levels of education of a couple. However, age was the only significant factor, with older couples tending to follow the more traditional roles.

Western standards, the number of divorces rose from almost 97,000 in 1970 to over 222,000 in 1997.

Social change has traditionally been slow in Japan, and it is unlikely that further changes in the role of women will be rapid, but the seeds are well established. In yet another way the distinctive culture of Japan will be influenced by that of the West.

AN AGEING SOCIETY

In recent years, population growth in Japan has slowed down. Low rates of infant mortality (children dying before the age of five) have reduced the need for large families. Social factors such as cramped living conditions and the high cost of housing have also led couples to have fewer children. This has caused the 'ageing' of Japanese society. The average age of the population is rising – estimates suggest that this will be 45 years by 2025, the highest of any developed country. The Japanese also have an extraordinary life expectancy. Men can expect to live to over 76 and women to nearly 83.

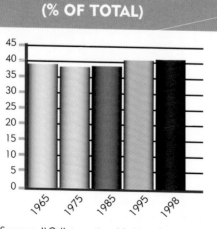

FEMALE LABOUR FORCE (% OF TOTAL)

Sources: ILO (International Labour Organisation)

SOCIAL INDICATORS

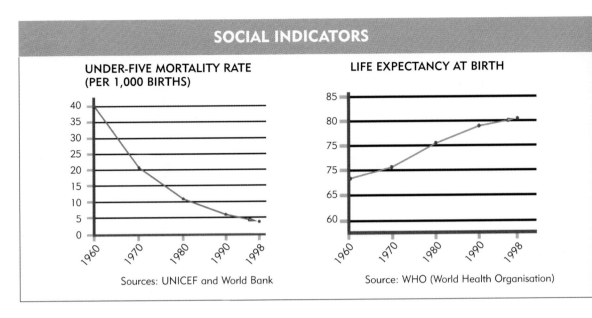

UNDER-FIVE MORTALITY RATE
(PER 1,000 BIRTHS)

LIFE EXPECTANCY AT BIRTH

Sources: UNICEF and World Bank

Source: WHO (World Health Organisation)

SOCIAL AND ECONOMIC IMPACTS

The ageing of Japanese society is destined to have serious social and economic impacts. The age of retirement may rise and some experts believe that there may be a shortage of labour. There will also be increasing demands on pension funds and health insurance schemes.

To combat these problems, the government is looking at a number of radical reforms. In respect of pensions these include raising the age at which people are eligible for pensions and placing more reliance on private pension schemes. Other suggestions include encouraging higher birth rates through family-friendly policies, providing incentives to encourage women and people over 60 to return to work, and allowing higher levels of immigration.

These issues are of particular interest to the young. They can no longer expect to have the comfortable retirements of previous generations. Whilst Japan is ahead of most countries in facing the problems of an ageing population, it is clear that its young people face yet more uncertainty in a rapidly changing world.

Japan's past successes have left a challenging legacy for these children growing up in an ageing society.

Decentralisation The outward movement of population, employment or similar functions away from an established central area or core.

Diet The Japanese parliament, comprising two chambers, the Lower House or House of Representatives and the Upper House or House of Councillors.

Disposable income The amount of income remaining after all expenses such as tax, rent and food costs have been met.

Dormitory town A town where many of the inhabitants travel to work outside the settlement itself.

Expressway A high-speed dual carriageway.

GDP Gross Domestic Product is the volume of goods and services produced annually in a country, but excluding earnings from overseas.

Geisha A professional woman especially trained to provide entertainment, conversation and company to a man or group of men. She will have skills as a hostess and, usually, in music and dancing.

Geothermal power Energy derived from the heat contained in rocks deep within the earth's crust or from hot springs or volcanoes.

GNP Gross National Product is the volume of goods and services produced annually within a country, which includes earnings from overseas.

HEP Hydroelectric power (HEP) is generated from running water falling through a gradient. Most HEP stations use dams to create a storage lake that will provide water all year round.

Infrastructure Communication systems such as roads and basic utilities such as electricity supplies that provide support to industry, services and residents.

Island arc A chain of volcanic islands created where an oceanic plate is being forced beneath a continental plate.

Karaoke Singing to a pre-recorded accompaniment, often in bars or clubs.

LEDCs Less Economically Developed Countries are those with relatively low incomes and limited economic development.

MEDCs More Economically Developed Countries are those with relatively high incomes and a high level of economic development.

Megalopolis An urban complex that encompasses many formerly separate cities. It derives from the Greek words for 'great' and 'city'.

Meiji Restoration The overthrow of the Tokugawan Shogunate by the Satsuma and Choshu clans in 1868. They restored the authority of the 14-year-old emperor, Mitsushito, and instituted a radical series of political, social and economic reforms that transformed Japan and opened it up to the West.

Monorails Tramway systems that use only one rail, which may be above or below the cabins.

Monsoon The seasonal change of wind direction that characterises the climates of many Eastern and South-east Asian counties.

Multiple cropping Harvesting more than one crop from the same plot of land.

Pachinko A game of pinball that is played on slot machines in large parlours throughout Japan.

Pacific Belt An extended zone of almost continuous urban and industrial development that stretches from Oita (Kyushu) to Ibaraki Prefecture (Honshu, east of Tokyo).

Recession A time when the level of economic activity declines, sometimes causing unemployment.

Reclaimed land Land that is reclaimed for human use from a natural habitat, for example the draining of marshland.

Referendum A vote on a single issue, such as nuclear power or whether to join the European Union.

Richter scale A scale used for measuring the size or energy release of earthquakes. The scale ranges from 1 to 10. Serious damage occurs around level 6.

Seismographs Sensitive instruments that record the intensity of earthquakes.

Shinkansen Japan's high-speed trains that run on dedicated tracks. There are currently four main lines stretching from Hakata in Kyushu to Akita in northern Honshu.

Shoguns A line or dynasty of military governors who ruled Japan from 1603 until 1868, when they were overthrown in the Meiji Restoration.

Smog Clouds of pollution that result from the action of sunlight on pollutants such as car exhaust fumes.

Tatami Mats used to cover the floors of Japanese houses. They are used as an official measure of house size and equal 1.8m by 0.9m.

Tectonic plates Sections or blocks of the earth's crust which 'float' like rafts on the underlying mantle. They move with respect to each other and the zones where they meet are prone to volcanic and earthquake activity.

Terraces Platforms cut into the sides of hills to make them suitable for agricultural use, especially the cultivation of rice.

Trade surplus The difference between the value of exports from a country and the value of its imports.

Tsunami Tidal waves or surges caused by earthquakes under the sea. When they reach land they can cause great devastation.

Typhoons Tropical storms resulting from systems of intense low pressure that form over warm, tropical seas and often move towards coastal areas where their high winds and violent rainfall can cause great damage.

FURTHER INFORMATION

BOOKS TO READ:

NON-FICTION:
Country Fact Files: Japan by John Baines (Hodder Wayland, 1998) Illustrated reference for KS2–3.

Country Insights: Japan by Nick Bornoff (Hodder Wayland, 1998) Illustrated reference for KS2.

Cultural Atlas of Japan by Martin Collcut, Marius Jansen and Isao Kumakura (Phaidon, 1998) Illustrated reference for KS3–4.

Economically Developed Countries: Japan by Lesley Downer (Hodder Wayland, 1998) Illustrated reference for KS3–4.

FICTION:
An Artist in a Floating World by Kazuo Ishiguro (Faber, 1986) A fictional account of some of the problems in post-war Japan.

WEBSITES:

ENVIRONMENT:
Japanese Environment Agency website:
www.env.go.jp/

GENERAL INFORMATION:
Useful information about Japanese lifestyle, geography and history:
www.jinto.go.jp/kidsweb/japan/a.html/

TOURIST INFORMATION:
Japanese Tourist Office:
www.cybercypher.com/japan/14/

MAGAZINES AND NEWSPAPERS:

Insight Japan A quarterly magazine that discusses modern Japanese issues in a clear way, with full-colour illustrations.

Japan Times An English language newspaper, available through specialist newsagents.

Nikkei Weekly An English language newspaper with a focus on business issues, available through specialist newsagents.

FILMS:

The Seven Samurai Directed by Akira Kurosawa. A classic film about samurai life (rated PG).

Tokyo Story Directed by Yasujiro Ozu. Often voted one of the ten best films ever made. A classic story of the clash of traditional and modern values in Japan (rated U).

Traditional architecture is often in harmony with the natural landscape.

Numbers shown in **bold** also refer to pages with maps, graphic illustrations or photographs.

A farmer sells her produce on the street.

Water, along with stone and plants, is an essential part of any Japanese garden.

61